Power Confessions

Volume One

Power Confessions

Volume One

Farley Dunn

◆◆◆ THREE SKILLET

POWER CONFESSIONS: VOLUME ONE, Dunn, Farley.
1st ed.

◖◕◖ THREE SKILLET

www.ThreeSkilletPublishing.com

ISBN: 978-1-943189-72-4

Table of Contents

Part 1:

I have Hope and Healing in Christ

I am healed by the wounds of Christ.

But he was pierced for our transgressions. He was crushed for our iniquities. The punishment that brought our peace was on him; and by his wounds we are healed.
Isaiah 53:5

My every need is satisfied through my Father God.

Yahweh is my shepherd: I shall lack nothing.

Psalm 23:1

I am restored in the presence of God.

He restores my soul. He guides me in the paths of righteousness for his name's sake. Psalm 23:3

My total trust is in the Master of Creation.

In the beginning, God created the heavens and the earth.

Genesis 1:1

My healing is perfected by the suffering of Christ.

Surely he has borne our sickness, and carried our suffering; yet we considered him plagued, struck by God, and afflicted.
Isaiah 53:4

I am the compassion of God to hurting people.

Put on therefore, as God's chosen ones, holy and beloved, a heart of compassion, kindness, lowliness, humility, and perseverance.
Colossians 3:12

I have a God who fights my battles for me.

You shall not fear them; for Yahweh your God himself fights for you.

Deuteronomy 3:22

God will turn all evil things to my good.

As for you, you meant evil against me, but God meant it for good, to bring to pass, as it is today, to save many people alive.
Genesis 50:20

I am filled with the strength and peace of God.

Yahweh will give strength to his people.
Yahweh will bless his people with peace.
Psalm 29:11

I find peace and rest in the shadow of the Almighty.

He who dwells in the secret place of the Most High will rest in the shadow of the Almighty.
Psalm 91:1

I am filled with hope through the power of the Spirit.

Hope doesn't disappoint us, because God's love has been poured out into our hearts through the Holy Spirit who was given to us.

Romans 5:5

I am encouraged unto hope through God's Word.

For whatever things were written before were written for our learning, that through patience and through encouragement of the Scriptures we might have hope.

Romans 15:4

I am called unto hope and the riches of His glory.

. . . Having the eyes of your hearts enlightened, that you may know what is the hope of his calling, and what are the riches of the glory of his inheritance in the saints.
Ephesians 1:18

My hope in Jesus is secure, for He is eternal and never fails.

[We have] hope of eternal life, which God, who can't lie, promised before time began.
Titus 1:2

I have the power to heal with signs and wonders.

*You stretch out your hand to heal; and . . .
signs and wonders [are] done through the
name of your holy Servant Jesus.*
Acts 4:30

I am weak, but through Christ I become strong.

He gives power to the weak. He increases the strength of him who has no might.
~ *Isaiah 40:29* ~

I can cast out every disease and sickness in the name of Jesus.

He called to himself his twelve disciples, and gave them authority over unclean spirits, to cast them out, and to heal every disease and every sickness.

Matthew 10:1

I am made whole by Jesus who was raised from the dead.

. . . In the name of Jesus Christ of Nazareth, whom you crucified, whom God raised from the dead, in him does this man stand here before you whole.

Acts 4:10

I am filled with understanding, power, counsel, and sound knowledge.

Counsel and sound knowledge are mine. I have understanding and power.
Proverbs 8:14

I am filled with the glory of God.

When the righteous triumph, there is great glory . . .

Proverbs 28:12

I am given power to do wonderous things by the authority of Jesus.

Now God raised up the Lord, and will also raise us up by his power.
1 Corinthians 6:14

I have a God who understands my weaknesses.

For in that he himself has suffered being tempted, he is able to help those who are tempted.

Hebrews 2:18

Through me, Jesus can do all things.

Looking at them, Jesus said, "With men this is impossible, but with God all things are possible."
Matthew 19:26

My blessing is already on the way.

Is anything too hard for Yahweh? At the set time I will return to you, when the season comes round, and Sarah will have a son.
Genesis 18:14

I am followed by the signs and wonders of the power of Jesus.

In the power of signs and wonders, in the power of God's Spirit; so that from Jerusalem, and around as far as to Illyricum, I have fully preached the Good News of Christ.

Romans 15:19

I am given power to change lives, even to the healing of the sick.

They even carried out the sick into the streets, and laid them on cots and mattresses, so that as Peter came by, at the least his shadow might overshadow some of them.
Acts 5:15

Every good thing is mine through my belief in Jesus.

Jesus said to him, "If you can believe, all things are possible to him who believes." Mark 9:23

I have intercession before God through the person of Christ.

Therefore he is also able to save to the uttermost those who draw near to God through him, seeing that he lives forever to make intercession for them.

Hebrews 7:25

I have seen the majesty of God and it is mine.

For we did not follow cunningly devised fables, when we made known to you the power and coming of our Lord Jesus Christ, but we were eyewitnesses of his majesty.

2 Peter 1:16

I am free from fear, for God is my strength and salvation.

Yahweh is my light and my salvation.
Whom shall I fear? Yahweh is the strength
of my life. Of whom shall I be afraid?
Psalm 27:1

I rejoice in whatever comes my way, for in Christ, I have hope.

Not only this, but we also rejoice in our sufferings, knowing that suffering produces perseverance; and perseverance, proven character; and proven character, hope.
Romans 5:3-4

I have a greater glory that will soon be revealed unto me.

For I consider that the sufferings of this present time are not worthy to be compared with the glory which will be revealed toward us.

Romans 8:18

I am perfect and complete through my endurance in Christ.

Let endurance have its perfect work, that you may be perfect and complete, lacking in nothing.

James 1:4

I am filled with the courage of Christ in all situations.

. . . Draw near today to battle against your enemies. Don't let your heart faint! Don't be afraid, nor tremble, neither be scared of them.
Deuteronomy 20:3

I live in daily victory through my Lord Jesus Christ.

But thanks be to God, who gives us the victory through our Lord Jesus Christ.
1 Corinthians 15:57

My trust is in the name of Christ my Lord.

Some trust in chariots, and some in horses, but we trust the name of Yahweh our God.
Psalm 20:7

I stand unafraid before my adversaries.

His heart is established. He will not be afraid in the end when he sees his adversaries.
Psalm 112:8

Jesus is Lord and Christ, sacrificed for me.

Let all the house of Israel therefore know certainly that God has made him both Lord and Christ, this Jesus whom you crucified.
— Acts 2:36

I receive every answer when I agree in prayer.

Again, assuredly I tell you, that if two of you will agree on earth concerning anything that they will ask, it will be done for them by my Father who is in heaven.
Matthew 18:19

My battles are already won, for God has defeated my enemy.

Yahweh will fight for you, and you shall be still.

Exodus 14:14

I am surrounded by an army of angels.

Don't be afraid; for those who are with us are more than those who are with them.
2 Kings 6:16

My God is bigger than those who are against me.

Yahweh thunders his voice before his army;
for his forces are very great; for he is strong
who obeys his command; for the day of
Yahweh is great and very awesome, and who
can endure it?
Joel 2:11

Part 2:

My Salvation is in Him

I am sanctified in Christ and called to be a saint.

To the assembly of God which is at Corinth; those who are sanctified in Christ Jesus, called to be saints, with all who call on the name of our Lord Jesus Christ in every place, both theirs and ours.

1 Corinthians 1:2

I am not my own but a temple of the Holy Spirit.

Or don't you know that your body is a temple of the Holy Spirit which is in you, which you have from God? You are not your own.

1 Corinthians 6:19

I am justified through the grace of Christ.

[We are] justified freely by his grace through the redemption that is in Christ Jesus.
Romans 3:24

I am redeemed through the blood of Christ.

In whom we have our redemption through his blood, the forgiveness of our trespasses, according to the riches of his grace.
Ephesians 1:7

My eyes are opened with the Good News of Christ.

In whom the god of this world has blinded the minds of the unbelieving, that the light of the Good News of the glory of Christ, who is the image of God, should not dawn on them.

2 Corinthians 4:4

I am now without sin through the Word of God.

Having been born again, not of corruptible seed, but of incorruptible, through the word of God, which lives and remains forever.

1 Peter 1:23

I believe on my Savior who died for me.

For God so loved the world, that he gave his one and only Son, that whoever believes in him should not perish, but have eternal life.
John 3:16

I am part of God's plan, and He is my salvation.

We know that all things work together for good for those who love God, to those who are called according to his purpose.

Romans 8:28

My children will walk in the footsteps of Jesus.

Train up a child in the way he should go,
and when he is old he will not depart from it.
Proverbs 22:6

I am the witness of Christ unto all the world.

Go, and make disciples of all nations,
baptizing them in the name of the Father and
of the Son and of the Holy Spirit.
Matthew 28:19

I shine in purity and righteousness through Christ.

If we confess our sins, he is faithful and righteous to forgive us the sins, and to cleanse us from all unrighteousness.

1 John 1:9

Jesus is greater than my sin and failures.

For all have sinned, and fall short of the glory of God.
Romans 3:23

I boast of Christ, my salvation and Lord.

[Our salvation is] not of works, that no one would boast.

Ephesians 2:9

I have the promise of eternal life in Christ Jesus.

For the wages of sin is death, but the free gift of God is eternal life in Christ Jesus our Lord.

Romans 6:23

I am redeemed through my confession in Christ.

If you will confess with your mouth that Jesus is Lord, and believe in your heart that God raised him from the dead, you will be saved.

Romans 10:9

I will live forever through Jesus, my resurrection.

Jesus said to her, "I am the resurrection and the life. He who believes in me will still live, even if he dies."

John 11:25

I am saved, not condemned; honored, not judged.

For God didn't send his Son into the world to judge the world, but that the world should be saved through him.

John 3:17

I am a guiding light to the world.

Even so, let your light shine before men; that they may see your good works, and glorify your Father who is in heaven.
Matthew 5:16

My redemption is in the Lord.

Israel, hope in Yahweh, for with Yahweh there is loving kindness. With him is abundant redemption.

Psalm 130:7

I will receive a great reward for my faithfulness.

His lord said to him, "Well done, good and faithful servant. You have been faithful over a few things, I will set you over many things. Enter into the joy of your lord."
Matthew 25:21

I live as Christ unto the world, the example of His hope and salvation.

. . . God was pleased to make known what are the riches of the glory of this mystery among the Gentiles, which is Christ in you, the hope of glory.

Colossians 1:27

I have the gift of life through the power of His resurrection.

That I may know him, and the power of his resurrection, and the fellowship of his sufferings, becoming conformed to his death.
Philippians 3:10

I am filled with the anointing to minister the gospel to the world.

The Spirit of the Lord . . . has anointed me to preach good news to the poor . . ., to deliver those who are crushed.
Luke 4:18

I am a minister of the Good News of the resurrected Christ.

Jesus returned in the power of the Spirit into Galilee, and news about him spread through all the surrounding area.
Luke 4:14

I speak salvation, and the power of God infuses my words with authority.

For God's Kingdom is not in word, but in power.

1 Corinthians 4:20

I am powerful through Christ crucified, for my strength flows from the cross.

For the word of the cross is foolishness to those who are dying, but to us who are saved it is the power of God.
1 Corinthians 1:18

I shout my salvation to the world, Good News! Good News!

For I am not ashamed of the Good News of Christ, for it is the power of God for salvation for everyone who believes; for the Jew first, and also for the Greek.

Romans 1:16

I am delivered from the clutches of the evil one.

But the Lord stood by me, and strengthened me, that through me the message might be fully proclaimed, and that all the Gentiles might hear; and I was delivered out of the mouth of the lion.

2 Timothy 4:17

I speak salvation and redemption through the authority of Christ.

They were astonished at his teaching, for his word was with authority.
Luke 4:32

I am delivered from every evil work and preserved for God's heavenly Kingdom.

And the Lord will deliver me from every evil work, and will preserve me for his heavenly Kingdom; to whom be the glory forever and ever. Amen.

2 Timothy 4:18

I reside in the hands of the One who holds creation in His grasp.

He is before all things, and in him all things are held together.

Colossians 1:17

I am quickened to life by the Spirit of the Holy God.

But if the Spirit of him who raised up Jesus from the dead dwells in you, he who raised up Christ Jesus from the dead will also give life to your mortal bodies through his Spirit who dwells in you.

Romans 8:11

I live in the power of the Spirit flowing through me.

My speech and my preaching were not in persuasive words of human wisdom, but in demonstration of the Spirit and of power.
1 Corinthians 2:4

I am the likeness of Christ through the redemption of the cross.

All things were made through him. Without him was not anything made that has been made.

John 1:3

My salvation is secured by the everlasting power of God.

By the power of God [you] are guarded through faith for a salvation ready to be revealed in the last time.

1 Peter 1:5

I live in Christ through my redemption on the cross.

He was in the world, and the world was made through him, and the world didn't recognize him.
John 1:10

I am chosen of Jesus, and He fills me with life.

For as the Father raises the dead and gives them life, even so the Son also gives life to whom he desires.

John 5:21

My flesh is put to death, and I live in righteousness before God.

Because Christ also suffered for sins once, the righteous for the unrighteous, that he might bring you to God; being put to death in the flesh, but made alive in the spirit.

1 Peter 3:18

No evil can come against me, for I am redeemed by the blood of Jesus.

Since then the children have shared in flesh and blood, he also himself in the same way partook of the same, that through death he might bring to nothing him who had the power of death, that is, the devil.

Hebrews 2:14

I bask in the light of Jesus, whom no man can know except through the Father.

[Jesus] alone has immortality, dwelling in unapproachable light; whom no man has seen, nor can see: to whom be honor and eternal power.

1 Timothy 6:16

I tread my enemies underfoot with Christ as my strength.

Through [Christ] will we push down our adversaries. Through your name, will we tread them under who rise up against us.

Psalm 44:5

God is my salvation; I lift my voice and rejoice.

The king rejoices in your strength, Yahweh!
How greatly he rejoices in your salvation!
Psalm 21:1

My salvation flows from the hand of the Almighty God.

. . . Don't be afraid. Stand still, and see the salvation of Yahweh, which he will work for you today . . .

Exodus 14:13

Part 3:

I am strong in my Faith in Jesus

I am filled with the truth of Christ.

But their minds were hardened, for until this very day at the reading of the old covenant the same veil remains, because in Christ it passes away.

2 Corinthians 3:14

Through Christ, I am redeemed.

*Because of him, you are in Christ Jesus,
who was made to us wisdom from God, and
righteousness and sanctification, and
redemption.*
1 Corinthians 1:30

I am triumphant through Christ.

Now thanks be to God, who always leads us in triumph in Christ, and reveals through us the sweet aroma of his knowledge in every place.

2 Corinthians 2:14

I have Christ in me, and I live by faith in Him.

I have been crucified with Christ, and it is no longer I that live, but Christ living in me. That life which I now live in the flesh, I live by faith in the Son of God, who loved me, and gave himself up for me.
Galatians 2:20

My goal is the high calling of God through Christ.

I press on toward the goal for the prize of the high calling of God in Christ Jesus.
Philippians 3:14

I stand in the presence of God.

But now in Christ Jesus you who once were far off are made near in the blood of Christ.
Ephesians 2:13

I have the peace of God.

To all who are in Rome, beloved of God, called to be saints: Grace to you and peace from God our Father and the Lord Jesus Christ.

Romans 1:7

I have spiritual understanding through the mind of Christ.

For who has known the mind of the Lord, that he should instruct him? But we have Christ's mind.

1 Corinthians 2:16

I live by the wisdom of Christ and the hope of His calling.

That the God of our Lord Jesus Christ, the Father of glory, may give to you a spirit of wisdom and revelation in the knowledge of him; having the eyes of your hearts enlightened, that you may know what is the hope of his calling, and what are the riches of the glory of his inheritance in the saints.
Ephesians 1:17-18

I walk in the light of the Lord.

For you were once darkness, but are now light in the Lord. Walk as children of light.
Ephesians 5:8

I have boldness and faith through my confidence in Christ.

In whom we have boldness and access in confidence through our faith in him.
Ephesians 3:12

I have a hope and a future in Jesus.

For I know the thoughts that I think toward you, says Yahweh, thoughts of peace, and not of evil, to give you hope and a future.
Jeremiah 29:11

I am surrounded by the Spirit of God.

Even though I walk through the valley of the shadow of death, I will fear no evil, for you are with me. Your rod and your staff, they comfort me.

Psalm 23:4

My eyes are focused on Christ alone.

[Love] doesn't behave itself inappropriately, doesn't seek its own way, is not provoked, takes no account of evil.
1 Corinthians 13:5

I am wise in God.

Trust in Yahweh with all your heart, and don't lean on your own understanding.
Proverbs 3:5

I walk together with the Lord.

God is our refuge and strength, a very present help in trouble.

Psalm 46:1

I am at peace in the presence of my enemies.

You prepare a table before me in the presence of my enemies. You anoint my head with oil. My cup runs over.

Psalm 23:5

Christ is my underpinning, and He never fails.

Love never fails. But where there are prophecies, they will be done away with. Where there are various languages, they will cease. Where there is knowledge, it will be done away with.

1 Corinthians 13:8

I am perfected in faith through Christ.

[We are] looking to Jesus, the author and perfecter of faith, who for the joy that was set before him endured the cross, despising its shame, and has sat down at the right hand of the throne of God.

Hebrews 12:2

My courage and strength flow from my faith in Christ.

Watch! Stand firm in the faith! Be courageous! Be strong!
1 Corinthians 16:13

My faith has made me pure through the cross.

For by grace you have been saved through faith, and that not of yourselves; it is the gift of God.

Ephesians 2:8

Jesus walks at my side.

. . . Behold, I am with you always, even to the end of the age.
Matthew 28:20

I am content in every situation.

Be free from the love of money, content with such things as you have, for he has said, "I will in no way leave you, neither will I in any way forsake you."
— Hebrews 13:5

My faith is the mustard tree, spreading its limbs over those I love.

Without faith it is impossible to be well pleasing to him, for he who comes to God must believe that he exists, and that he is a rewarder of those who seek him.

Hebrews 11:6

I am filled with faith through the Word of God.

So faith comes by hearing, and hearing by the word of God.
Romans 10:17

My plans and dreams in Christ are guaranteed.

Also delight yourself in Yahweh, and he will give you the desires of your heart.
Psalm 37:4

I am sheltered in God, my fortress and high tower.

Yahweh is my rock, my fortress, and my deliverer; my God, my rock, in whom I take refuge; my shield, and the horn of my salvation, my high tower.
— Psalm 18:2

I have a secure future in my mighty God.

Indeed surely there is a future hope, and your hope will not be cut off.
Proverbs 23:18

The Lord listens and hears my every need.

Then those who feared Yahweh spoke one with another; and Yahweh listened, and heard . . .
Malachi 3:16

My God goes before me to prepare my way.

He will go before him in the spirit and power of Elijah, 'to turn the hearts of the fathers to the children,' and the disobedient to the wisdom of the just; to prepare a people prepared for the Lord.
Luke 1:17

I have a stronghold against the enemy through the power of Christ.

. . . The children of Israel made themselves the dens which are in the mountains, and the caves, and the strongholds.

Judges 6:2

I am mighty in the righteousness of Christ.

Better is a little that the righteous has, than the abundance of many wicked. For the arms of the wicked shall be broken, but Yahweh upholds the righteous.

Psalm 37:16-17

I am covered by the protecting hand of God.

The wicked watches the righteous, and seeks to kill him. Yahweh will not leave him in his hand, nor condemn him when he is judged.
Psalm 37:32-33

I am wise through faith and filled with the power of God.

Your faith [stands not] in the wisdom of men, but in the power of God.

— 1 Corinthians 2:5

I am strong in faith and able to perform all He asks of me.

Yet, looking to the promise of God, he didn't waver through unbelief, but grew strong through faith, giving glory to God, and being fully assured that what he had promised, he was also able to perform.
— *Romans 4:20-21*

I stand on the everlasting Rock, and I will trust in Him forever.

Trust in Yahweh forever; for in Yahweh is an everlasting Rock.

Isaiah 26:4

I claim the power of God as my right in Him.

For the invisible things of him since the creation of the world are clearly seen, being perceived through the things that are made, even his everlasting power and divinity; that they may be without excuse.

Romans 1:20

I walk in power through the gift of the cross.

No one takes [my life] away from me, but I lay it down by myself. I have power to lay it down, and I have power to take it again. I received this commandment from my Father.
John 10:18

My heart rejoices in the soon return of the Son of Man.

Then they will see the Son of Man coming in clouds with great power and glory.
Mark 13:26

I overflow with strength through my time in prayer.

Seek Yahweh and his strength. Seek his face forever more.
1 Chronicles 16:11

I walk in the shadow of my fortress God, and my footsteps in Him are sure.

God is my strong fortress. He makes my way perfect.

2 Samuel 22:33

I receive the Word of God as His inviolate truth for my life.

Now these [Jews] were more noble than those in Thessalonica, in that they received the word with all readiness of the mind, examining the Scriptures daily to see whether these things were so.

Acts 17:11

I am prosperous through my strength and courage in Christ.

Then you will prosper, if you observe to do the statutes and the ordinances which Yahweh gave Moses concerning Israel. Be strong and courageous. Don't be afraid, and don't be dismayed.

1 Chronicles 22:13

I am not burned, neither am I scorched, for the Lord is my protector.

When you pass through the waters, I will be with you; and through the rivers, they will not overflow you. When you walk through the fire, you will not be burned, and flame will not scorch you.

Isaiah 43:2

Power Confessions

Get all three individual *Power Confessions* books today!

Volume One:

Hope and Healing

Salvation

Faith

Volume Two:

Overcoming

Power in Christ

Resisting the Devil

Volume Three:

I am a Child of God

New Life in Him

Praise and Thanksgiving

Power Confessions: Collection

Contains all three books in one volume!

All *Power Confessions* volumes are available at Three Skillet Publishing and on Amazon.